# TAMPA BAY BUCCANEERS

BRENDAN FLYNN

# WWW.APEXEDITIONS.COM

Copyright © 2025 by Apex Editions, Mendota Heights, MN 55120. All rights reserved. No part of this book may be reproduced or utilized in any form or by any means without written permission from the publisher.

Apex is distributed by North Star Editions:
sales@northstareditions.com | 888-417-0195

Produced for Apex by Red Line Editorial.

Photographs ©: Doug Murray/AP Images, cover, 1; Alex Menendez/AP Images, 4–5, 58–59; Kevin Sabitus/Getty Images Sport/Getty Images, 6–7, 36–37, 42–43, 52–53; Focus On Sport/Getty Images Sport/Getty Images, 8–9, 19, 54–55; Vernon Biever/AP Images, 10–11, 22–23; Sylvia Allen/Getty Images Sport/Getty Images, 12–13; Scott Audette/AP Images, 14–15; Al Bello/Getty Images Sport/Getty Images, 16–17; Ronald C. Modra/Getty Images Sport/Getty Images, 20–21; Andy Lyons/Getty Images Sport/Getty Images, 24–25; Al Messerschmidt/Getty Images Sport/Getty Images, 26–27; Matt Stroshane/Getty Images Sport/Getty Images, 29; Doug Benc/Getty Images Sport/Getty Images, 30–31; Streeter Lecka/Getty Images Sport/Getty Images, 32–33; Kevin C. Cox/Getty Images Sport/Getty Images, 34–35; Peter Joneleit/AP Images, 39, 57; Mike Zarrilli/Getty Images Sport/Getty Images, 40–41; Cliff Welch/Icon Sportswire, 44–45; Shutterstock Images, 46–47; George Gojkovich/Getty Images Sport/Getty Images, 48–49; Mike Carlson/Getty Images Sport/Getty Images, 50–51

**Library of Congress Control Number: 2024940174**

**ISBN**
979-8-89250-160-6 (hardcover)
979-8-89250-177-4 (paperback)
979-8-89250-301-3 (ebook pdf)
979-8-89250-194-1 (hosted ebook)

Printed in the United States of America
Mankato, MN
012025

## NOTE TO PARENTS AND EDUCATORS
Apex books are designed to build literacy skills in striving readers. Exciting, high-interest content attracts and holds readers' attention. The text is carefully leveled to allow students to achieve success quickly.

# TABLE OF CONTENTS

CHAPTER 1
## GO BUCS! 4

CHAPTER 2
## EARLY HISTORY 8

PLAYER SPOTLIGHT
## LEE ROY SELMON 18

CHAPTER 3
## LEGENDS 20

PLAYER SPOTLIGHT
## DERRICK BROOKS 28

CHAPTER 4
## RECENT HISTORY 30

PLAYER SPOTLIGHT
## MIKE EVANS 38

CHAPTER 5
## MODERN STARS 40

CHAPTER 6
## TEAM TRIVIA 48

TEAM RECORDS • 56
TIMELINE • 58

# CHAPTER 1

# GO BUCS!

It's a beautiful Sunday afternoon in central Florida. Fans enter the stadium. Many are wearing red jerseys. Others wear light orange. They're all cheering for the Tampa Bay Buccaneers. Soon, it's time for the game to start.

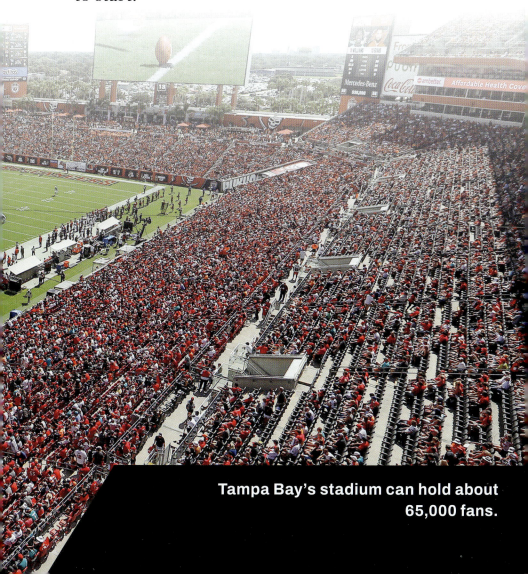

Tampa Bay's stadium can hold about 65,000 fans.

Mike Evans scores a touchdown during a 2023 game against the Jacksonville Jaguars.

In the second quarter, Buccaneers quarterback Baker Mayfield fires a pass. Receiver Mike Evans hauls it in. It's a touchdown! The crowd goes wild. But the Bucs aren't done yet. Later in the quarter, Mayfield and Evans connect for another score. Tampa Bay rolls to an easy win.

## CREAMSICLE UNIFORMS

Tampa Bay's original jerseys were often called Creamsicle uniforms. They were light orange. That's the same color as the ice cream treat. The Bucs wore light orange until 1997. These days, the team uses Creamsicle jerseys as throwback uniforms.

# CHAPTER 2

# EARLY HISTORY

The Tampa Bay Buccaneers joined the NFL in 1976. They were one of two expansion teams. The Seattle Seahawks also entered the league that year. The Bucs got off to a rough start. They didn't win a single game in their first season.

**Quarterback Steve Spurrier (11) led Tampa Bay's offense in the team's first season.**

Tampa Bay's second season wasn't much better. The Bucs lost their first 12 games. The team was on a 26-game losing streak. That set an NFL record. Finally, the Bucs beat the New Orleans Saints in Week 13. It was their first-ever win. The Bucs won their next game, too. They finished the season 2–12.

### FIRST COACH

John McKay began his career as a college coach. He led the University of Southern California. McKay helped the team win four national titles. In 1976, he became Tampa Bay's head coach. McKay spent nine seasons with the Bucs.

Running back Ricky Bell (42) looks for an opening during a 1977 game against the Green Bay Packers.

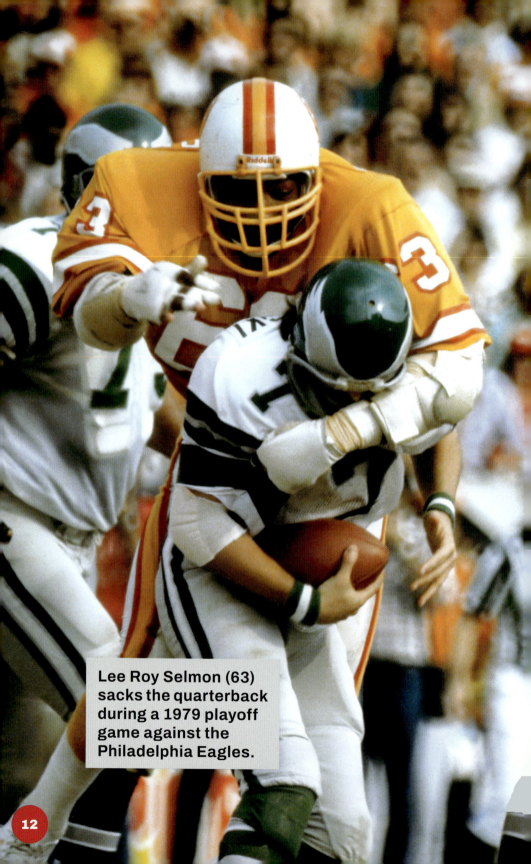

Lee Roy Selmon (63) sacks the quarterback during a 1979 playoff game against the Philadelphia Eagles.

In their third season, the Bucs improved to five wins. Then, in 1979, they shocked the NFL. The Bucs put together a 10–6 record. They won their division. They even made it to the conference title game. But the magical run ended there. The Bucs lost 9–0 to the Los Angeles Rams.

## ONE AND DONE

The Buccaneers made it back to the playoffs in 1981 and 1982. But both times, they lost in the first round. Both losses were to the Dallas Cowboys. Bucs fans didn't have much to cheer about after that. The team didn't return to the playoffs for 15 years.

In the late 1990s, Tampa Bay was on the rise. From 1997 to 2001, the Bucs reached the playoffs four times. In 1999, they returned to the conference title game. But once again, they lost to the Rams. The next two years, the Bucs were knocked out in the first round.

## BUILDING SUCCESS

Tony Dungy started his coaching career as a defensive assistant. Tampa Bay gave him his first head coaching job in 1996. Dungy turned the Bucs into winners. However, the team fired him after the 2001 season. He later led the Indianapolis Colts to a Super Bowl title.

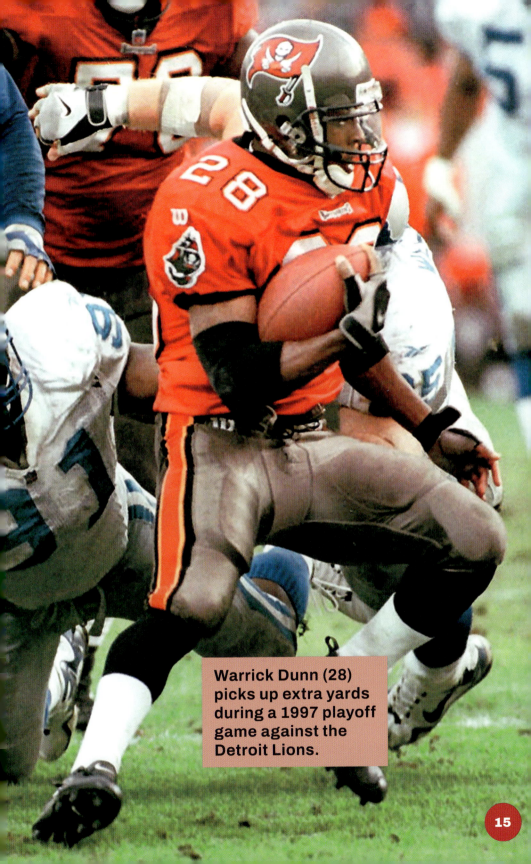

Warrick Dunn (28) picks up extra yards during a 1997 playoff game against the Detroit Lions.

Jon Gruden took over as Tampa Bay's head coach in 2002. In his first season, the team had the NFL's top defense. The Bucs reached the conference title game. They beat the Philadelphia Eagles 27–10. With that win, they made it to the Super Bowl. In the big game, Tampa Bay faced the Oakland Raiders. That was Gruden's former team. The Bucs crushed them 48–21. It was Tampa Bay's first title.

Defensive tackle Warren Sapp (99) celebrates a sack during the Super Bowl.

## PLAYER SPOTLIGHT

# LEE ROY SELMON

Lee Roy Selmon was the Buccaneers' first-ever draft pick. Selmon played defensive end. He was quick and powerful. Selmon helped the Bucs win two division titles. In 1977, Selmon racked up 13 sacks. That was a career high.

Selmon spent his entire nine-year career with Tampa Bay. During that time, he made the Pro Bowl six times. Injuries forced him to retire. He was just 30 years old. But he was voted into the Pro Football Hall of Fame in 1995.

**IN 1979, SELMON WAS NAMED NFL DEFENSIVE PLAYER OF THE YEAR.**

# CHAPTER 3

# LEGENDS

Doug Williams was Tampa Bay's top draft pick in 1978. The quarterback had a great arm. During his rookie year, Williams earned the starting job. Then in 1979, he led the Bucs to their first division title.

Doug Williams threw for more than 12,000 yards in his five seasons with the Bucs.

James Wilder (32) exploded for 1,544 rushing yards in 1984.

Running back James Wilder spent nine years with Tampa Bay. His best season came in 1984. He set an NFL record with 407 runs. He also caught 85 passes. Wilder piled up 2,229 total yards that year.

Quarterback Vinny Testaverde was the first pick in the 1987 draft. He started for Tampa Bay for five seasons.

### THE SELMON BROTHERS

Defensive end Lee Roy Selmon was a star at the University of Oklahoma. So was his brother, linebacker Dewey Selmon. They both joined the Bucs in 1976. The brothers spent five years together in Tampa Bay.

Mike Alstott (40) thundered his way to six straight Pro Bowls from 1997 to 2002.

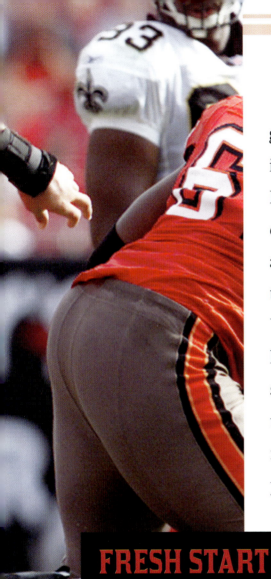

Tampa Bay had two great running backs in the late 1990s. Fullback Mike Alstott caught passes, blocked, and scored lots of touchdowns. Tailback Warrick Dunn was lightning-quick. Dunn spent six seasons with the Bucs. He gained more than 1,000 total yards in all of them.

## FRESH START

Quarterback Brad Johnson spent several years with the Minnesota Vikings. He mostly served as a backup. In 2001, Johnson arrived in Tampa Bay. The Bucs relied on their strong defense. They just needed a quarterback who could protect the ball. Johnson did that. He threw only six interceptions in 2002.

Tampa Bay was all about defense in the early 2000s. Defensive tackle Warren Sapp was a tireless pass rusher. Linebacker Derrick Brooks was a tackling machine. Passing against the Bucs was never easy. Ronde Barber's strong play at cornerback was a big reason why. Safety John Lynch starred as well.

## FIERCE LINEBACKER

In 1993, Hardy Nickerson joined Tampa Bay. He recorded 214 tackles that year. That led the NFL. He remained the Bucs' top linebacker for much of the 1990s.

Ronde Barber (20) returns an interception for a touchdown during a 2006 game against the Eagles.

## PLAYER SPOTLIGHT

# DERRICK BROOKS

Derrick Brooks joined Tampa Bay in 1995. He was selected in the first round of the draft. The linebacker played for 14 years. He didn't miss a single game. But Brooks was more than just reliable. He was also an excellent tackler.

The 2002 season may have been his best. That year, Brooks intercepted five passes. He scored four touchdowns. And he was named Defensive Player of the Year. Brooks ended the season with yet another big play. He came through in the Super Bowl. He returned an interception for a touchdown.

**BROOKS MADE THE PRO BOWL 11 TIMES IN HIS 14-YEAR CAREER.**

# CHAPTER 4
# RECENT HISTORY

After the Super Bowl win, Jon Gruden stayed with the Bucs for six more seasons. He helped them win two more division titles. But both times, Tampa Bay lost in the first round of the playoffs. That led to another long drought. The team went 12 seasons without reaching the playoffs.

Bucs quarterback Chris Simms (2) dives for a touchdown during a playoff game against Washington in the 2005 season.

The Bucs went through several head coaches after Gruden left. But none of them could lift the team back to the top. The best season in that era came in 2010. That year, the Bucs went 10–6. But they had just one more winning season the rest of the decade.

## BOTTOMING OUT

The Bucs hit rock bottom in 2014. They lost 11 of their final 12 games. However, the team earned the top pick in the next year's draft. Tampa Bay used it to select quarterback Jameis Winston.

Quarterback Josh Freeman led Tampa Bay's offense in the early 2010s.

The Bucs got a huge boost in 2020. That year, Tom Brady joined the team. The quarterback had been a star on the New England Patriots. He'd won six titles there. He came to Tampa looking for another.

Brady led the Bucs all the way to the Super Bowl. In the big game, Tampa Bay's defense shut down the Kansas City Chiefs. The Bucs rolled to a 31–9 victory. It was their second title.

Tom Brady earned the Super Bowl MVP Award in Tampa Bay's win over the Chiefs.

After the 2022 season, Brady retired. Baker Mayfield took over at quarterback. In 2023, he led Tampa Bay to a division title. In the first round of the playoffs, the Bucs crushed the Eagles 32–9. Tampa Bay lost in the next round. But fans hoped it wouldn't be long before the team was back on top.

## GRONK'S RETURN

Tight end Rob Gronkowski spent several years with Tom Brady in New England. Gronkowski retired after the 2018 season. But after one year away, he joined Brady in Tampa Bay. Over the next two years, Gronkowski caught 100 passes.

Baker Mayfield escapes from a defender during the Bucs' playoff win over the Eagles.

## PLAYER SPOTLIGHT

# MIKE EVANS

The Buccaneers selected Mike Evans with their first pick in the 2014 draft. The wide receiver stood 6-foot-5 (196 cm). So, he towered over most defenders. He was also blazing fast.

Bucs quarterbacks quickly learned a lesson. They just had to throw the ball near Evans. He would usually make the play. Evans started his career with 10 straight 1,000-yard seasons. No player in NFL history had done that before. In five of those seasons, Evans made the Pro Bowl.

**IN 2023, EVANS LED THE NFL WITH 13 TOUCHDOWN CATCHES.**

# CHAPTER 5

# MODERN STARS

Jameis Winston became Tampa Bay's quarterback in 2015. He started for five seasons. He became the team's all-time passing leader.

Tom Brady took over in 2020. Many fans think Brady was the greatest quarterback in NFL history. He made a good case for that in 2020. He was 43 years old. But he still led the Bucs to a Super Bowl win.

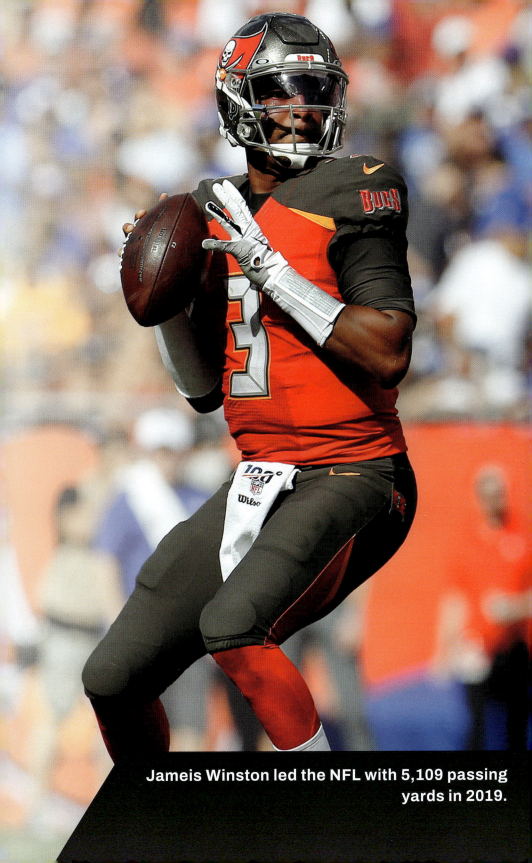

Jameis Winston led the NFL with 5,109 passing yards in 2019.

Chris Godwin topped 1,000 receiving yards in four of his first seven seasons.

Mike Evans became Tampa Bay's top receiver. But he wasn't the team's only great pass catcher. Chris Godwin joined the Bucs in 2017. He posted 1,000 receiving yards in four of his first seven seasons. And in 2022, he hauled in 104 catches.

## STRONG START

Tristan Wirfs got his career off to a great start. The offensive tackle was a rookie in 2020. The team drafted him to protect Tom Brady. Wirfs made his first Pro Bowl in 2021. And he didn't stop there. He earned Pro Bowl nods again in 2022 and 2023.

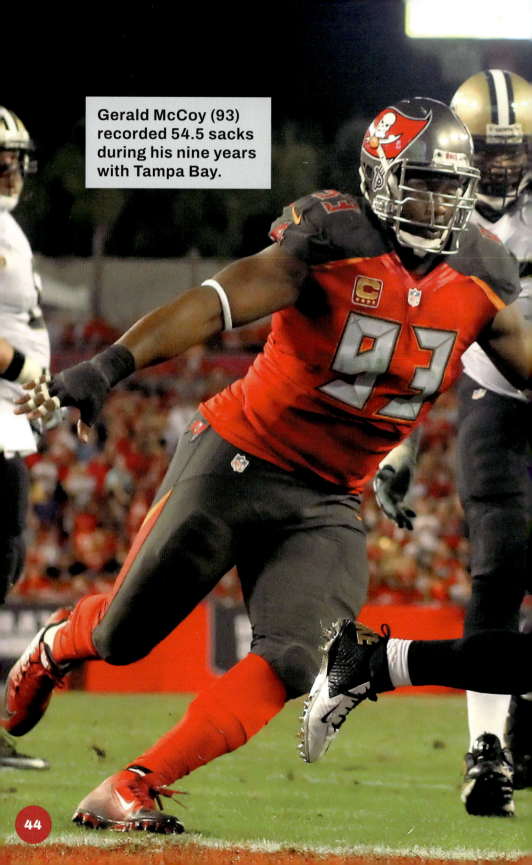

Gerald McCoy (93) recorded 54.5 sacks during his nine years with Tampa Bay.

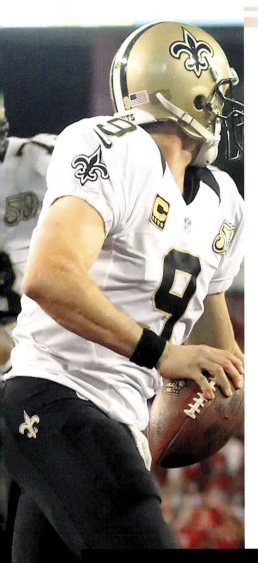

Defensive tackle Gerald McCoy arrived in Tampa Bay in 2010. He stayed with the Bucs until 2018. Over that time, he made six Pro Bowls. McCoy was tough against the run. But he was quick enough to rush the passer, too.

## BETTER WITH AGE

Defensive end Simeon Rice joined the Bucs in 2001. He was already a star. He'd recorded 51 sacks over five years with the Arizona Cardinals. But Rice got even better in Tampa Bay. In his first five seasons with the team, he averaged 13.5 sacks per year.

In the late 2010s and early 2020s, Tampa Bay had strong linebackers. Shaquil Barrett racked up 19.5 sacks in 2019. Rookie Devin White also excelled that year. He continued to record lots of tackles in the years to come. And Lavonte David made more than 1,400 tackles over 12 years.

## SUPER ROOKIE

Bucs safety Antoine Winfield Jr. followed in his father's footsteps. The elder Winfield spent 14 years in the NFL. But he never won a Super Bowl. The younger Winfield needed only one season to do it. As a rookie, he made six tackles in the Super Bowl. He also grabbed an interception.

Shaquil Barrett (58) chases Buffalo Bills quarterback Josh Allen during a 2021 game.

# CHAPTER 6

# TEAM TRIVIA

Wins were hard to come by in the Bucs' early years. Head coach John McKay needed a way to get through it. So, he relied on a good sense of humor. He became famous for his jokes after losses. One time, a reporter asked him about the team's execution. McKay supposedly said, "I'm in favor of it."

John McKay had three winning seasons in his nine years leading the Buccaneers.

The Buccaneers have made plenty of rivals over the years. Since 2002, Tampa Bay has shared a division with three teams. They are the Atlanta Falcons, Carolina Panthers, and New Orleans Saints. Florida also has two other NFL teams. They are the Miami Dolphins and the Jacksonville Jaguars.

## CHANGING PLACES

The Buccaneers spent many years in the NFC Central Division. It didn't make much sense, though. The other four teams were based in the Upper Midwest. The NFL created new divisions in 2002. Now, Tampa Bay is part of the NFC South.

Rachaad White (1) runs the ball during a 2023 game against the Panthers.

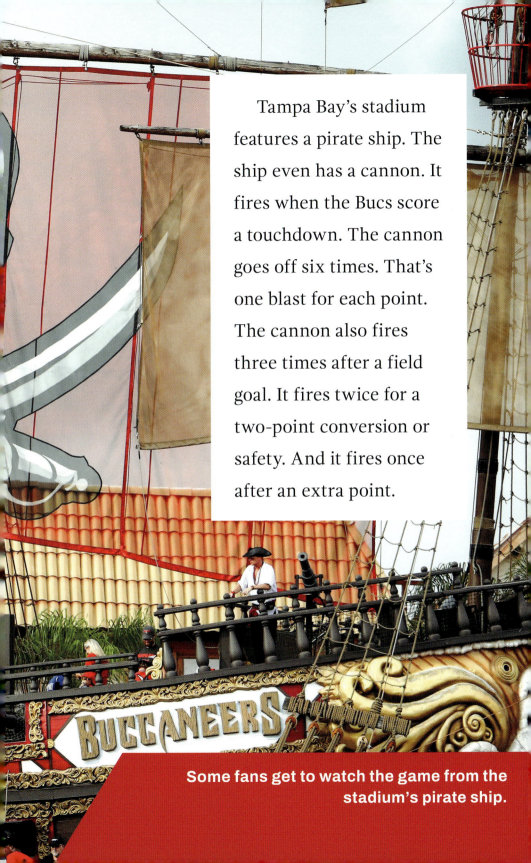

Tampa Bay's stadium features a pirate ship. The ship even has a cannon. It fires when the Bucs score a touchdown. The cannon goes off six times. That's one blast for each point. The cannon also fires three times after a field goal. It fires twice for a two-point conversion or safety. And it fires once after an extra point.

Some fans get to watch the game from the stadium's pirate ship.

In 2002, the Bucs took part in an odd trade. They gave the Raiders several draft picks. They also gave up $8 million. In return, the Bucs received head coach Jon Gruden. It's rare for a head coach to be traded. But it worked out for Tampa Bay. Gruden led the Bucs to a Super Bowl win over his old team.

## HOMETOWN WIN

In the 2020 season, Tampa Bay hosted the Super Bowl. The Buccaneers ended up winning the title that season. So, they won the Super Bowl in their home stadium. They were the first team to do so. However, more than half of the seats were empty. The NFL limited crowd sizes due to COVID-19.

Jon Gruden led the Bucs to the playoffs three times in seven seasons.

55

# TEAM RECORDS

**All-Time Passing Yards:** 19,737
Jameis Winston (2015–19)

**All-Time Touchdown Passes:** 121
Jameis Winston (2015–19)

**All-Time Rushing Yards:** 5,957
James Wilder (1981–89)

**All-Time Receiving Yards:** 11,680
Mike Evans (2014–)

**All-Time Interceptions:** 47
Ronde Barber (1997–2012)

**All-Time Sacks:** 78.5*
Lee Roy Selmon (1976–84)

**All-Time Scoring:** 592
Martin Gramatica (1999–2004)

**All-Time Games Played:** 241
Ronde Barber (1997–2012)

**All-Time Coaching Wins:** 57
Jon Gruden (2002–08)

**Super Bowl Titles:** 2
(2002, 2020)

*Sacks were not an official statistic until 1982. However, researchers have studied old games to determine sacks dating back to 1960.*

*All statistics are accurate through 2023.*

# TIMELINE

**1976** — The Tampa Bay Buccaneers join the NFL as an expansion team. They become the first team in the Super Bowl era to finish a season winless.

**1977** — The Bucs beat the New Orleans Saints and St. Louis Cardinals to end their second season on a two-game winning streak.

**1979** — In their fourth season, the Bucs win their division. In the playoffs, they make it all the way to the conference title game.

**1984** — John McKay, the team's original head coach, leaves the team.

**1997** — Second-year head coach Tony Dungy leads the Bucs back to the playoffs.

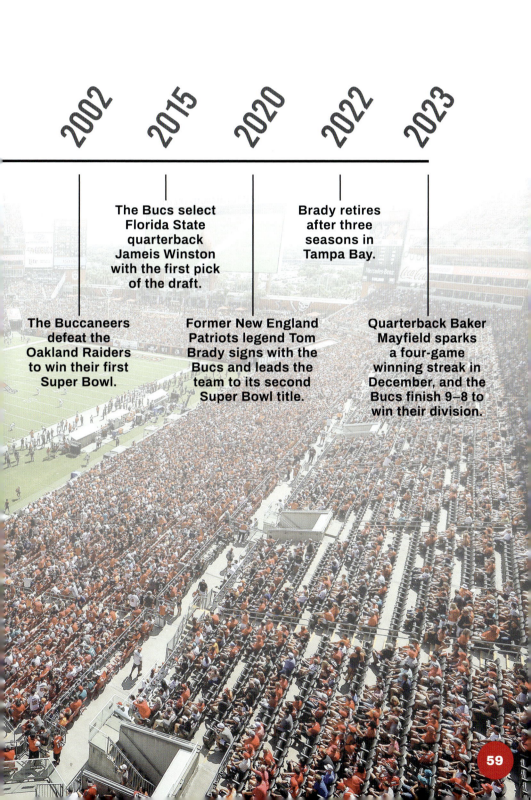

**2002** — The Buccaneers defeat the Oakland Raiders to win their first Super Bowl.

**2015** — The Bucs select Florida State quarterback Jameis Winston with the first pick of the draft.

**2020** — Former New England Patriots legend Tom Brady signs with the Bucs and leads the team to its second Super Bowl title.

**2022** — Brady retires after three seasons in Tampa Bay.

**2023** — Quarterback Baker Mayfield sparks a four-game winning streak in December, and the Bucs finish 9–8 to win their division.

59

# COMPREHENSION QUESTIONS

*Write your answers on a separate piece of paper.*

1. Write a paragraph that explains the main ideas of Chapter 2.

2. Who do you think was the greatest player in Buccaneers history? Why?

3. Who had at least 1,000 receiving yards in each of his first 10 seasons?
   A. Chris Godwin
   B. Mike Evans
   C. Rob Gronkowski

4. Why was Tampa Bay's 1979 division title so shocking?
   A. It was the team's first season in the NFL.
   B. The team's starting quarterback had been hurt all year.
   C. The team had been very bad in its first three seasons.

**5.** What does **reliable** mean in this book?

*The linebacker played for 14 years. He didn't miss a single game. But Brooks was more than just **reliable**. He was also an excellent tackler.*

    **A.** dependable, or always able to play

    **B.** strong, or very good at tackling

    **C.** injured, or not able to play

**6.** What does **drought** mean in this book?

*That led to another long **drought**. The team went 12 seasons without reaching the playoffs.*

    **A.** a time without success

    **B.** a full football season

    **C.** a playoff victory

*Answer key on page 64.*

# GLOSSARY

**conference**
A group of teams that make up part of a sports league.

**division**
In the NFL, a group of teams that make up part of a conference.

**draft**
A system that lets teams select new players coming into the league.

**execution**
How well a team plays. *Execution* can also mean putting someone to death as a penalty for a crime.

**expansion team**
A new team that is added to a league.

**interceptions**
Passes that are caught by a defensive player.

**league**
A group of teams that play one another and compete for a championship.

**rookie**
An athlete in his or her first year as a professional player.

**sacks**
Plays that happen when a defender tackles the quarterback before he can throw the ball.

**throwback**
Something that returns to the way it was in the past.

# TO LEARN MORE

## BOOKS

Chandler, Matt. *Football's Greatest Hail Mary Passes and Other Crunch-Time Heroics.* North Mankato, MN: Capstone Press, 2021.

Coleman, Ted. *Tampa Bay Buccaneers All-Time Greats.* Mendota Heights, MN: Press Box Books, 2022.

Holleran, Leslie. *Tom Brady: Gridiron G.O.A.T.* Minneapolis: Lerner Publications, 2024.

## ONLINE RESOURCES

Visit **www.apexeditions.com** to find links and resources related to this title.

## ABOUT THE AUTHOR

Brendan Flynn is a San Francisco resident and an author of numerous children's books. In addition to writing about sports, Flynn also enjoys competing in triathlons, Scrabble tournaments, and chili cook-offs.

# INDEX

Alstott, Mike, 25

Barber, Ronde, 26
Barrett, Shaquil, 46
Brady, Tom, 34, 36, 40, 43
Brooks, Derrick, 26, 28

David, Lavonte, 46
Dungy, Tony, 14
Dunn, Warrick, 25

Evans, Mike, 7, 38, 43

Godwin, Chris, 43
Gronkowski, Rob, 36
Gruden, Jon, 16, 31–32, 54

Johnson, Brad, 25

Lynch, John, 26

Mayfield, Baker, 7, 36
McCoy, Gerald, 45
McKay, John, 10, 48

Nickerson, Hardy, 26

Rice, Simeon, 45

Sapp, Warren, 26
Selmon, Dewey, 23
Selmon, Lee Roy, 18, 23

Testaverde, Vinny, 23

White, Devin, 46
Wilder, James, 23
Williams, Doug, 20
Winfield, Antoine Jr., 46
Winston, Jameis, 32, 40
Wirfs, Tristan, 43

## ANSWER KEY:
1. Answers will vary; 2. Answers will vary; 3. B; 4. C; 5. A; 6. A